ESCAPE THE FRIENDZONE

SEDUCE HER FROM FRIEND TO LOVER IN 5 STEPS OR LESS

Robert Belland

BOBAIR MEDIA INC
Edmonton, Alberta, Canada

Dedicated to my female friends for giving me a lifetime of insights and love!

Robert Belland /BOBAIR MEDIA INC
Edmonton, Alberta, Canada
robert@bobair.com

Escape The Friendzone / Robert Belland. —1st ed.
ISBN 978-1-927449-08-0

CONTENTS

"Action is the foundational key to all success."

—Pablo Picasso

INTRODUCTION

INTRODUCTION

THIS ENTIRE BOOK IS dedicated to my fellow brothers who have somehow found themselves lost in the wasteland we call The Friendzone!

If you're reading this book, then you're probably a dude who's somehow made friends with a hottie, but can't seem to get any romantic traction going with her.

You've found yourself trapped in The Friendzone.

And now you're looking for some advice on how to escalate the relationship from being "just friends" to being **more** than just friends.

Maybe you want to be friends with benefits? That's cool. I can help you with that.

Maybe you're in love? That's cool too. I'm gonna help you with that as well.

Maybe you simply have a crush and you want to start dating her to see where it goes? Well, that's much more levelheaded, and I can help you too.

For anyone else, here's a quick explanation. The Friendzone is the sad, depressing purgatory between being strangers and being passionate lovers. Like finding a perfectly cooked pizza on your dining room table that you can see and smell, but you're not allowed to touch or taste. And yes women, if you're reading this, sometimes we see you like a delicious meal we want to devour.

I think most women don't get this idea of "The Friendzone," because being close friends with guys already has its own payoff for them: emotional connection, sharing, being emotionally intimate, receiving constant attention and approval. These things tend to be a big focus for women in their romantic relationships too, so getting these payoffs without having to manage the messy drama that sex brings to the table is a no-brainer for them.

But we guys get it. Finding a woman who's awesome to hang out with **and** who's hot is a killer combo. What's better than being able to have sex with a close friend of the opposite sex (or the same sex if that's your style).

But let's first take a second to appreciate where you're at! There's something wonderful about having a girl who's just a friend. Because she's more likely to be honest with us about how we look, what we say, and how we act. Whereas someone we're trying to date is more likely to be on her best behaviour and more likely to ignore the weird shit we do and say.

So before we go racing down the "how do I seduce my friend" road, I should cover three main points for you to understand before moving forward in this book.

FIRST

Realize something really important here: as you start to go down this road of seduction, you need to realize that you're making a very important decision, and this is something **you** need to decide for yourself.

I've done this myself, so I know what I'm talking about.

I don't mean to sound dramatic, but this is important: You need to decide that you're so committed to making things happen with this girl and that you're willing to sacrifice your current relationship as it now stands.

What I mean is that no matter how well things go, or how bad things end up, your relationship with her is going to change. Maybe you're going to become much more romantically involved.

Or maybe you're going to push her away without meaning to.

There's a million ways this might play out, but **for sure** your relationship with her will be different.

If you're trying to sleep with a woman who's only ever been just a friend, then you already know you want to redefine this relationship... and that's perfectly cool! I'm just saying, take a moment to recognize your situation. You're happy but you want more, and "more" requires risk and effort on your part.

So make this decision consciously.

And honestly.

And openly with yourself.

I've stood in that same place myself a few times over the years, where I'm good friends with a woman and I've decided to try to make more of it. And I recognized that I needed to make myself accountable and responsible for what I was choosing to do, which was to take action and attempt to move my relationship with her to new more exciting, maybe even more sexual, places.

Even at the risk of losing her entirely.

So first, take note of what you're actually doing here. You're consciously deciding to take responsibility for the relationship you have with this woman so that you can make it better and direct it towards what you want, while also accepting that she may ultimately want something different. And you must first accept this before moving forward. This way you're prepared, but more importantly you'll stop wasting time hesitating and being fearful. The road ahead has a million positive outcomes, but it's full of unknowns and it'll probably feel scary. And until you decide for yourself, you'll stay stuck where you are with her.

SECOND

Let's be honest here: **escaping The Friendzone is almost entirely about sex.** Otherwise you wouldn't care about The Friendzone. You'd just stay close intimate friends and you wouldn't be reading this book.

So I'm not going to waste much time pretending this topic is about dating or marriage or whatever. It's not only possible, but probable that if you start sleeping with this girl, you'll automatically also be dating her.

I once heard this saying, and it's really true: *"If you want to make a girl your girlfriend, then simply start sleeping with her."*

That sounds simple, and it's true. I've rarely slept with a woman who didn't also want to date me.

It's possible, and those wonderful women do exist, but it's rare.

So recognize this: if your goal is to sleep with her, accept that the consequences are that she's going to be really into you and will want to also date you from that point forward. If your goal isn't to date her, then you'll need to recognize that fact and make it **very** clear to her before you're both naked.

And that's COMPLETELY fine!

"Friends with benefits" is totally okay when both parties know that's the deal. I'll mention the differences in approach throughout this book. But for the most part, this book is about turning her from a friend into a lover and a girlfriend.

Many of the steps are identical, so even if "friends with benefits" is your goal, the tips in this book will help.

THIRD

Believe it or not, if you're already close friends with her, you've done all the hard work! You're past her guards, she's lowered her defences, and she already thinks you're kind of cool.

That's a blessing and a curse.

Because she already has her first impression of you, and you can't change that. And that's okay. We must accept that. And now you must accept that what you've been doing up to this point has helped you become friends, but has also hindered your progress to be more than friends. So in order to change how she thinks, and most importantly how she **feels** about you, you're also going to have to change how you think and how you feel about yourself.

This is the hardest part of seducing a woman: **changing our own bad habits.**

Because who you are is who you are, you can't change that.

But how you **think**, what you **believe**, how you **feel** and how you **behave** are all within your control!

If you're going to move forward through this book, you need to accept that what I'm going to be suggesting is probably going to feel challenging for you. Because if you were already doing these things naturally, you wouldn't be reading these words.

I'm going to be challenging your beliefs a little and challenging you to act differently, while also explaining to you how to stay true to yourself so that you're still authentically you, which is most attractive to her.

So now, what's your best way forward?

Keep reading, take notes, and most important **take the actions** I suggest. The rest of this book will be about how you can seduce her, without scaring her away or ruining the current relationship.

If at any time you have questions, don't hesitate to contact me directly: *robert@bobair.com* .

STEP 1:
STOP WHAT YOU'RE DOING

A romantic relationship needs both rapport and attraction.

Rapport is about connection. It's about sameness. It's about being friends. We have the most natural rapport with our family and close friends because we share the same values, beliefs and experiences. We feel cozy being around people who think and feel like us because it feels safe and we feel "un-judged", like being "home." And up to this point in your relationship with her, you've been building this connection, this rapport. And that's awesome! Except the only feelings you're inspiring in her are feelings of comfort, safety and connection.

Here's what you're missing:

Attraction!

Friction.

Tension.

Emotional unease.

Mystery.

Suspense.

Sexual chemistry!

You see, **attraction is almost the opposite of rapport.** It's about teasing, and flirting, and playfully pushing her away. And attraction works best when there's the opposing feeling of rapport and connection.

The magic of **pushing her away while also pulling her in.** That's the definition of sexual chemistry.

I explain this concept explicitly in my six-hour online video course *Get the Girl*, but it's worth saying again here:

It doesn't matter what she **thinks** of you, it only matters how she **feels** when she's with you.

SCENARIO

Imagine a scenario: you're at the bar with this girl, you're having drinks and you're sharing stories with each other about growing up. You're really connecting and it feels awesome. And then a guy comes over from across the room and introduces himself to the woman you're with, while completely ignoring that you exist. He's in a leather jacket, maybe he's got some tattoos, and ultimately you can tell he's kind of cocky and arrogant, and someone we might label a "Bad Boy."

She seems flattered and annoyed at the same time. He compliments her on her beautiful hair, but then teases her about her lack of tattoos. And as she's about to brush him off, he excuses himself back to his seat at the bar where two other girls are fawning all over him.

Overall, you are annoyed because he was rude and obnoxious and you can't wait to make fun of him with your friend. But she's blushing and looking over at him while ignoring your rant. And then she looks at you and says, *"Yeah, that guy sure likes himself, eh?"* But for the rest of the night she's ignoring you and looking over at him, waiting for him to look at her.

And now you're feeling frustrated and confused because you've already proven how awesome a guy you are, how you listen and pay attention and how you care and connect. And yet in one second she's distracted by this new guy who was rude and dismissive.

What the hell is going on?!

Why do girls like "Bad Boys"?

Well, here's the truth: healthy, happy women don't like bad boys. But they will often find them attractive for sexual reasons. Maybe kind of like how we guys will find so-called "slutty girls" attractive while also not wanting to date them. We can't help how we feel.

Attraction isn't a choice that we make - our bodies and emotions have their own agendas. And so when a Bad Boy pushes her buttons, there's nothing she can do about it. The difference is that healthy, happy women don't act on these initial feelings, and those feelings just fade away without being given any second thought.

Unhealthy women, on the other hand, will give those feelings way too much importance and will chase these guys as way of chasing those feelings of excitement and sexual energy.

Bad Boys are like junk food: they taste great at first, but leave women feeling ill and full of regret. But man, does she love that sugar rush!

The good news is that **you** can create all of these same triggers in her without being an asshole or a Bad Boy.

That's mostly what this little book is about: building her attraction and feelings of sexual desire for you. But before we get into that, you need to stop doing a few things that are ruining your chances with her.

1) STOP TELLING HER YOUR EVERY THOUGHT AND FEELING.

The biggest mistake guys make when they are trying to escape The Friendzone that is they try to convince her to like them by telling her how much they like her first. We guys are too logical. We think, *"If only she knew how much I liked her, and all of my feelings for her, like in the movies, then she'll start to think like me!"*

Except this doesn't work. For endless reasons, but the most important being this: attraction isn't a choice. It's not about logic.

You can't change how she thinks, but you **can** change how she **feels.**

Seduction is a game.

And it starts with **you**.

And when you're being fun, it makes her want to play too.

Think of it like this: if you're playing poker and you tell everyone what's in your hand, then nobody will want to play because knowing your hand is boring. So telling her how you feel about her all the time does two horrible things:

- It makes you seem like an emotional girl. No offence to emotional women, because emotional women are women and women are my favorite! But she's already a woman. And if you want to turn her on, you need to remind her that you're a **man.**

- When she knows what you're thinking and feeling, it takes away all of the mystery. It takes you off her mind, leaving her to go about her life thinking about other stuff. It ruins the tension. It ruins the mystery. But when you're a closed book and a mystery, she'll go home and wonder. There will be this seed in her mind, like a loose thread she'll want to play with. Maybe she'll be sitting around wondering what you're thinking and feeling. Maybe not, but at least you can give her the space to be uncertain about what you're thinking and feeling, and that uncertainty is the key to helping build her interest.

So no love letters, no long text messages or drunk phone calls professing your love. Stop all of that immediately.

2) STOP HANGING OUT WITH HER LIKE SHE'S "JUST A BUDDY."

At least for the moment, stop doing all of the "buddy" stuff you typically do. You can go back to that once you're dating or sleeping together, but for now, stop.

This little book is entirely about you reframing yourself from being her buddy to becoming a "sexual threat." Now, when I say "sexual threat" I don't mean that you're threatening or that she's fearful of being raped. I mean that currently, as buddies, she sees you as non-sexual. Instead, you really need her to be

17

sexually charged up by you, so that she's realizing that she's in danger of wanting to sleep with you.

Typically, we guys see sex differently than women do. Women **love** sex and want sex as much as we guys, but they are way more at risk when they engage in sex!

- They can get pregnant, which is a huge risk.

- They can be raped or physically assaulted,

- They're at risk of social judgement (no girl wants to be labeled a slut, for example).

So even just sleeping with a guy one time can have all types of consequences for her. Her sexual urges can be threatening to her, and that's just not something we guys typically appreciate or acknowledge!

And so when a woman has sexual feelings, she has to juggle a complexity of emotions and risks that we guys don't. But ultimately, being on her sexual radar is the goal. Being a sexual option is what we're after.

Moving forward, stop what you're doing and take a break. Give her some space. Don't make any new plans to hang out. I'll give you direction on what to do in the next chapter.

3) DON'T EXPLAIN WHY YOU'RE BEING DIFFERENT.

For example, don't text her and say, *"Hey, we can't hang out this week. I'm trying to make myself a sexual option for you now."*

Or whatever. You get it.

If she asks, *"Hey, why can't we hang out?"* or *"Why do you seem so distant?"*, just play it cool and say, *"Wuuuuut? Nah, I'm just busy this week."*

She will probably feel like you're being different as you move forward, but that's the point. Don't confirm or deny, just be aloof. Be a mystery. **And always be playful.** Because she never wants to think you're doing anything to manipulate your relationship. And obviously manipulation isn't our objective.

Our initial goal is to make a change in you, and because of that she'll naturally feel different when interacting with you.

And that's a good thing.

You're not trying to be an asshole, you're just shifting gears.

4) STOP SHOWERING HER WITH ATTENTION, GIFTS, COMPLIMENTS, AND AFFECTION.

You can't buy her love through these kind of gifts anyway. They are only meant for a girl you're already dating seriously, not someone you're trying to seduce.

So stop it all.

It'll feel like you're giving her the cold shoulder at first, because you kind of are, but it's temporary. Our goal here is to start communicating with her unconscious feelings, so we don't need to waste too much time on the words you're saying to her. So stop saying them for now.

5) START SAYING NO.

Up until this point you're probably a yes man. We all say yes too often as a type of social lubricant. As a way of making things easy. As a way of making people like us. And that's all about rapport, and we don't care about rapport right now, we only care about **attraction**.

So stop saying yes and start saying no.

Even if you want to say yes.

For example, she texts you, *"Hey, I have an extra ticket, come with me to this concert."* You say, *"No."*

Then wait.

Then follow up with, *"You come with ME to this concert. But bring the tickets. Tell me what time the show is so that I know when to come pick you up."*

Realize you're texting like this in a playful sarcastic tone, not a domineering bossy tone. You're not trying to control her. You're just role playing where you're the leader and she's the follower.

But there are plenty of good times to say no. Like, *"Hey, can we hang out this Friday night?"* to which you can say, *"No, I can't that night."*

See? You're creating space and you're saying no.

NO is one of those **magic** words.

Like **LOVE** or **FUCK**.

It has **power**.

So use it.

STEP 2:
GET EDUCATED

You need to learn about women and dating and you need to learn about **attraction**.

I'm not going to get into the ridiculous details needed to completely understand the foundations of attraction, because you can get all of that from my online video course *Get the Girl* (check the last page of this chapter for free access to my online video course), but I'll give you some basics to get you started.

You've already shown that you're a cool enough dude to hang out with. Your rapport skills are probably pretty decent already. But before you start working on flirting and teasing her, make sure you've done your homework.

It's your job to **learn**.

Constantly.

Endlessly.

Forever.

And I don't just mean reading books, listening to podcasts and consuming online courses (but I do mean those things as well). I mean going out and gaining life experience by interacting with women, feeling nervous, feeling successful, feeling shy, feeling horny, and learning **in your physical body** what it feels like to flirt with women.

There's an old saying that goes like this: you don't know something until you do it. Learning from a book is powerful for the brain, but only once you're doing it will you really get it!

> *"You do not really understand something unless you can explain it to your grandmother."*
> *~ Albert Einstein*

Learning about attraction, flirting, teasing, and amping up her sexual interest should be number one on your agenda right now.

Listen dude... this is a huge world. There are many, many other men out there trying to get with all of the available women.

And that might sound like there's a scarcity of available women, but there's not. And that's because 99% of the men in this world will never pick up a book that teaches them the powerful psychology of sexual attraction. Therefore, **it's tragically easy to get ahead of the next guy** by simply picking up a couple books and getting educated.

Your job is to get so familiar with attraction that you can teach it to your buddy who's terrible with women. You need to get completely **obsessed** with learning about attraction, seduction and dating.

Read my book *Ignore and Score*, as a good start.

Read David DeAngelo, David Deida, and Neil Strauss next. They will give you the deepest, most epic understandings of attraction.

Why focus so deeply on attraction?

Because up to this point, you've been completely neglecting it with this woman. Otherwise you wouldn't be in The Friendzone.

I'll tell you a secret about The Friendzone: it's basically a waiting room for guys who haven't yet had the guts to flirt and escalate. Flirting is just another word for building attraction.

Just like the word *teasing*. Growing up, I thought teasing was about hurting someone's feelings, but think back to the playground when a boy liked a girl. In order to get her attention, he would pull her hair, or push her in the dirt and run away laughing.

When your intent is to **be playful** and to **make her laugh**, then you're starting in the right place when it comes to teasing. Flirting and teasing and building attraction are all about pushing her emotional buttons.

It's about getting an emotional response.

Because getting the girl is all about how she **feels**. And so, in order to develop her sexual interest you must turn her on emotionally. You must have an impact on her body. Being nice and friendly doesn't do that. Being friendly is about comfort. Being attractive is about reaction, tension and friction, with a sexual intent.

While you're getting yourself more educated on this idea of attraction, you'll begin to realize that building attraction is like pumping up a bike tire. You have to pump up and down. We call this **push/pull**.

You push the pump down and it inflates the tire slightly. Then you pull the pump handle back up in preparation for more air. And you repeat. **This push and pull is what flirting is.**

What's happening is that you tease her playfully (which is almost like you're pushing her away) and then you make her laugh or make her feel good with a sincere compliment (which emotionally pulls her back in).

Push her away, then pull her back in.

Back and forth.

Building attraction is basically foreplay.

It's all foreplay. It's all preparation that should be getting her excited to be with you, to kiss you, and to have sex with you.

One of the most important aspects of success comes from our willingness to learn something new. So sit yourself down and force yourself to get educated on building attraction. Because you're not going to inspire her to feel differently about you if you're the same guy.

You need to become the guy who **gets it**.

The guy who finally understands what's going on behind the scenes. The guy who can see the Matrix, so to speak.

Building attraction isn't about logic, which is why we guys don't get this aspect automatically. We have to sit down and learn it, then go out and practice it. Because inspiring her feelings through your own playfulness takes knowledge and then it takes practice.

Realize something: women start learning about attraction as teenagers reading magazines about chasing boys, teasing boys, flirting, makeup, style, clothes, and ways to get a guy's attention. They will put in 10,000 hours of research on what makes a guy tick by the time you've discovered a book like this one.

So don't feel dumb for not getting this automatically. It's perfectly normal to need to read about attraction before understanding it. So give yourself a break. And sit down and get educated on attraction and other dynamics like push and pull.

Now, with that all said, I'll be honest with you here. I'm telling you to go read about attraction and get yourself educated, but the truth is that you could skip this step entirely if you had to. Because understanding how attraction works isn't going to make you attractive. Only through your actions and behaviours will you actually find success with her.

But I'm recommending this step first because if you were willing to take action naturally, you would have by now. So in order to help get your head right I'm suggesting you get educated first, as a foundation and as a starting point, so that when you're finally ready to take action you take the **right** action.

STEP 3: LEADING

Purgatory.

The biggest reason you're in this purgatory with this woman is because you've not taken action. You're not **leading** this relationship anywhere. Instead you're sitting back admiring her and letting her lead.

That's it.

If you skipped all the steps in this book and only did one thing, it should be this: **TAKE ACTION!**

What you've failed to understand is that women aren't attracted to you because of what you're doing or saying, but because of who you're **being**.

You need to start being attractive instead of being friendly.

Odds are you've ended up following her around like a little puppy dog. Following a girl puts her in the leadership role and she simply can't be attracted to a follower. She might love a puppy and want to give it attention, but she's not going to want to spend a long romantic night between the sheets with a puppy.

She wants a **man**.

A **leader**.

You must learn to take the lead, and only then will there be a chance that she'll follow you.

TAKING ACTION

Here's one of the best-kept secrets I've ever learned when it comes to being confident with women, and pay attention, because I'm serious: **only through action do we gain confidence.**

Here's why. Let's say you take action, you cross that crowded room and you talk to that pretty girl. You took action, took a risk, and now you're experiencing the fallout of that action. You're experiencing what happens when you do what you did.

OUTCOME ONE

She likes what you've done and you two hit it off. And ultimately you learn that what you did (crossing that room, taking that risk) was the right thing to do, and the next time you're in a similar situation, you're going to have a little more confidence because of your experience.

OUTCOME TWO

But what if things go badly? What if she laughs and makes fun of you and you embarrass yourself? Then you look at what you did, and you feel proud of yourself for facing your fears and using courage to take action. That's what a man does. And your friends will pat you on the back for being brave in the face of your fears. And you can tell your friends that story, which you can look back at and laugh, because our embarrassing stories are our best stories!

And, when you take the time to learn from that experience, you'll remember whatever it is that you said that missed the mark with her, or the obvious red flags that should have told you to not bother with that specific woman. In any case, you'll have a new experience under your belt, which will give you a little more confidence the next time you're in that same situation because you'll be slightly more prepared thanks to your experience.

Do you see what I'm saying?

Your experience makes you slightly more prepared the next time you face the same situation, therefore you're going to be slightly more confident. Because every time we take action, we can learn from it and grow.

Every time we do nothing and we let our fears dictate our results, we're left feeling less sure, more anxious and more of a victim of our circumstances.

So **always** take action.

That's how leading works. Leading isn't about always being right and never making mistakes. Leading is about making mistakes as fast as possible in order to get better, stronger, braver and more successful.

Success with women only comes to those willing to fail over and over again in pursuit of what they desire.

This is one reason why some guys lose their girlfriends: they stop leading and they start letting her lead.

We harm our romantic relationships when we waste time with questions like, *"Well, where do you want to eat? I'm happy eating anywhere, how about you decide?"*

She's just like you, she doesn't want to think or decide. So instead, take the pressure off her, and **you** decide. If she doesn't like your choice, she'll say so.

LEADING

Attraction is about tension, flirting and sexual danger, while rapport is about sameness, connection, and loosening the tension. The error we make, as guys in The Friendzone, is that we fear that if we try to escalate we'll upset the delicate balance and possibly ruin the relationship.

We say things to ourselves like, *"I can't try to kiss her because she'll freak out and it'll ruin how she sees me, and I just don't want to take a risk like that with this woman I care so much about!"*

Except this is mostly bullshit.

What we're not willing to say is that we're scared. Maybe we're really thinking, *"If I take a crazy chance like this and I try to come on to her, she's going to realize I'm a creepy weirdo who's secretly been planning on kissing her since we first met, and I'm going to be humiliated and never hear from her again, and she's going to tell all of our closest friends how messed up I am..."*

Basically, every fear we have bubbles to the surface and we stop ourselves from doing anything. We become paralyzed by our own imagined fears and scenarios.

But I'm here to save you from all of this.

I'm here to tell you the facts of your situation.

Here's the truth you're not seeing...

THE TRUTH

You two are friends. FRIENDS! You should be able to take a shit on her carpet and still recover with an apology and shared laughs. I mean, think of all the dumb shit you've fought with your guy friends about, and all the stupid things you've done while drunk and then had to apologize for later.

There's almost nothing you can't recover from when you sincerely apologize.

Trust me on this. Women have grown up with guys constantly trying to kiss them. They've experienced it. It's not the trauma you're imagining it is.

So let me plant that seed in your head right now: it's okay to try to kiss this girl.

Maybe not yet, because you still need to grow her sexual interest, but eventually she's going to want you to kiss her. And you're going to have to.

This is what leading is about. **It's about taking action.** The ideas of attraction are all just ideas until you take action.

When you take action, you're building attraction. And that's where the gold is.

So what do I mean when I say "leading"?

If you've gone through my section on leading in my *Get the Girl* video course, then you'll be pretty familiar with this by now, but in summary, here's the basics: **Leading is about confidently, and playfully, taking action and moving your relationship forward.**

From emotional escalation (that's sharing secrets, being vulnerable and open, and overall being close friends) to physical intimacy (that's about touch and physical contact).

In a more literal sense, leading might just be something as simple as walking over to a woman, smiling at her and saying hello.

Or maybe it's sending a text to your girlfriend and telling her that you're taking her to a surprise location for dinner, and to be ready in 30 minutes.

Or maybe it's holding her hand to help her out of the car.

Or maybe it's that warm hug hello and goodbye.

Maybe it's cuddling on the couch while watching a movie.

Maybe it's whispering something funny in her ear, with your hot breath down her neck.

And why is this attractive? Because attraction is about tension, movement and action. The word "action" is right there at the end of the word attraction.

And when you look and smile and move and talk, you're expressing your personality and your authority.

And you're leading.

And we humans naturally tend to follow the leader.

Your every movement displays how you feel about yourself. And how you feel about her. And ultimately how we feel infects how others feel when they're with us. When we're nervous and insecure and too scared to act, that's us displaying a lack of courage, which her body might read as cold. She'll want to avoid those feelings.

Instead, if you're confident, you'll stand up straight, you'll make healthy and happy eye contact, and you'll speak with clear authority. Our mannerisms and body language give us away. They can't be hidden with fancy pick-up lines or an expensive car.

BEING AUTHENTIC

I really think the key to being good with women comes from being our authentic selves. Women are naturally attracted to men who **are who they are**.

You see, when a guy is nervous and insecure and is too shy to say what he really thinks and feels, he's not being himself. Instead, he's in his own head, trying to act and behave in a certain way to manipulate how others see him. He's constantly worrying what other people think. And women will be turned off by this naturally, because that guy will seem unsafe, or like he's hiding something, or like he has some secret about himself that he doesn't want the world to know.

Maybe we call him shy, but really it's just a dude with ego issues. Because it's our ego that makes us shy or makes us cocky, both of which are attempts to control how others see us.

The magic happens when we tune out our ego, and instead accept that people will believe what they want and that it's none of our business how they see us. And in turn, if we can tune out our inner thoughts and worries and instead experience the moment as it is, then suddenly we act more natural and confident as a result. And even if we're sometimes an asshole by being too honest, at least people respect that.

This is why you need to sit your ass down and talk to yourself man to man. I realize this may seem a little intense or psychotic or delusional or whatever. But I guarantee that there is a part of your conscious and unconscious mind that thinks it's **not** okay to be turned on by this woman, and so you've been hiding your true feelings up to this point.

This is a **huge** mistake.

So let me take this moment to give you permission to be a man with sexual desire and feelings.

It's **okay** to have sexual feelings for her or any other woman you find attractive. It's perfectly natural for your body to be attracted to whatever it's attracted to.

If you like skinny girls, that's fine.

If you like fat girls, that's fine.

If you like this friend of yours, that's fine!

If you like some friend's hot wife, that's all fine!

The key is discretion when it's appropriate, and calibration. For example, if you're married, it's not appropriate to be eyeballing other women in front of your wife or other people.

Pay attention here: **It's okay to have sexual feelings, but it's not always okay to freely act on them.** For example, when the woman is married, or you're married. Or even if you're just passing her on the street.

I think the mistake we guys make is that we'll meet some hottie while living our life, and we'll obsess about her after she's long gone as a way of recreating that intense sexual vibe we felt when we met her. That's a mistake and harmful to us. The key is to allow the feelings to exist, and then allow them to exit naturally, without a desperate teenage attachment to holding onto those feelings.

I think we guys need to give ourselves permission to be sexual creatures and have sexual feelings, but also have enough modesty and self-esteem to let go of those feelings instead of chasing them like teenage boys.

I suggest we accept them as they happen, and then let them go.

Don't get so attached.

Give yourself permission to be a sexual creature. It's okay to desire someone and to express that desire when it's appropriate. It stops being appropriate when either of you are not single, or perhaps the age difference is not appropriate, or if she's made it clear she's not interested.

When it comes to you and this female friend, my guess is that you've been waiting for her to say, *"It's okay to flirt with me"*, but here's a reality check:

First, she's never going to do that.

Second, that's you asking her to lead.

You have to lead.

And you do that by testing her boundaries in a fun and playful way. What I learned from Jack Tripper, from Three's Company in the '80s, is that it's okay to find women hot and attractive as long as you respect their boundaries, and as long as they don't mind the attention. And if you're harmless and playful, she's going to find you fun and funny. Believe me, I've said some of the most inappropriate things imaginable and have never had my face slapped.

Again, it's okay to find this woman attractive. And it's okay to show her how you feel. And I'll say this again: don't waste time telling her how you feel, because in telling her you're really just trying to get a feel for where she's at. Like saying, "Oh, you look nice" and then waiting for her to say the same thing.

It's needy.

But acting on your feelings? That's leading.

So if you're turned on by her, and your body craves her, and you also care for her in a way that implies that you would never hurt her, then you're displaying both a hunger for her (and women love being the object of desire if the man is attractive) and you're displaying an ability to restrain yourself by staying cool.

This displays that you'd be a good lover - full of passion but able to control yourself. She's already lived a life full of horny guys who lack self-control and who lack action. So when she's already friends with you, she's going to have her guard down, and she's already going to know she can trust you not to hurt her. This is the perfect sandbox for flirting and playful sexual energy.

Now it's your turn to lead her into a place she hasn't felt with you, or perhaps hasn't felt comfortable expressing with you.

A sexy place. A place of sexual desire and passion.

And leading doesn't mean you're the alpha of the room, or that you can lead men into battle. It's much less intense than this. It's about leading ourselves. And it's about leading her. When a guy is nervous but is still willing to walk across a room to talk with a woman he doesn't know, that displays his courage in the face of his fears. That's a huge turn on for a woman. And so, with this woman in your life, leading has these same impacts on her emotional body.

When you lead her, her impulse will be to follow you.

When you treat her like a friend, she's going to follow that lead.

Her instinct will be to follow your lead, so if you stop leading her into The Friendzone she'll stop putting you there. If instead you start leading her down the "let's be lovers" road, she'll follow you there too.

And so leading will now be all about you.

You set the tempo. You set the date, the time, the location, when you're going to pick her up and drop her off.

You could even suggest what she wears. I'll get into more detail in the last step of this mini-course, but for now prepare yourself to be the driver, the leader, the decider.

STEP 4:
MEET OTHER WOMEN

At first this seems counterintuitive, but it's not.

It's **powerful**.

One reason you might be stuck on this girl is because you're suffering from "oneitis." The deadly disease that causes you to only have passion for one woman because you've fooled yourself into thinking she's unique, special and one-of-a-kind.

If you've placed this girl on a pedestal, you've basically screwed yourself. Because no woman can look down on a man from up on a pedestal and feel attracted to him. Women want to look up to a man.

Think of it like this. Let's say you're chasing her and she's playfully running away. Ultimately, she would have to stop running and settle to be with you. She'd have to decide there's no better option and simply settle for you.

Come on! That's horrible!

That's not her fantasy.

Her fantasy is to be chasing a guy and to eventually catch him!

And in order to be that guy she's chasing, she has to put you on the pedestal. Which is completely within reason, you just haven't given her a chance or a reason to do that yet. Step one of this mini-book is all about taking her off the pedestal so that she won't feel like she's better than you, and hopefully she'll feel like she might be losing you.

You're giving her the gift of missing you *(stolen from David DeAngelo)*.

And now she needs to playfully earn back your attention, so to speak.

And there's nothing as good at helping us regain our perspective on this one woman as meeting other women worth getting to know.

You see, **in isolation we lose perspective**. This is one of the major reasons we get depressed or feel anxiety. We allow ourselves to become isolated, and in our isolation our negative thoughts and feelings become distorted. And it's this distortion that fuels bad decisions.

And so, if you value this one woman so highly that you're not dating other women, you've lost perspective.

It's simply not healthy to chase a woman you're not actually dating, in my opinion. So in order to regain perspective, and to help give you your balls back, you need to go meet more women and date them. Because there are three magical things that happen when you do this:

1) You suddenly get that female attention you deserve and have been craving.

This helps you relax more when you're interacting with the one you're trying to seduce, because you're not going to be all needy or hungry for her. Instead you're going to be relaxed and maybe even a little distracted.

This is gold.

This is the zone you should always be in. Like the clear mind and body that we feel during that 10 minutes after an orgasm. Just relaxed and loose, instead of pent up and anxious and wound up tight.

2) To get the girl, you have to be able to get all the girls.

You see, when you're getting regular practice at being fun and flirty with other women, this sharpens your skills at being good with that one special girl. Plus it's a nice distraction. It'll pull you out of your obsession with that one girl.

3) You dating other women offers her the opportunity to feel jealous.

When she realizes other women want you, your value climbs dramatically. It's really that simple.

I've seen this happen with my own female friends. As soon as I'm busy dating other women, suddenly they text me more, they flirt more, and they simply are more fun to be around. It's a natural thing for women to be competitive, and it works in your favour.

Here's an extra bonus: It's entirely possible you'll meet someone worth dating exclusively.

Let's not discount the idea that you could actually find someone amazing while you're out there dating. And really, that's the point, isn't it? I mean sure, this girl that's a "friend" is probably awesome, which is why you're so into her. But ultimately, if someone else that's awesome comes along and shows interest, that's really where your energy should go.

So go out and practice your dating skills, and especially your escalation skills. Your ability to take a woman by the hand, lead her to her table, lead her from across the table to the seat next to you, and lead her from whispering a secret in your ear to making out with you in the back of a restaurant, is the kind of skill that will get you the girl!

STEP 5

STEP 5:
ESCALATE

Let me tell you a little story about how I first realized the basics of this five-step process.

Many years ago I was good friends with this hot little lady. We hung out a lot but nothing really came of it because we were both in other relationships at the time. And as a side note, I tend to really like having female friends, more so than any other guy friends I have actually. Even when I was growing up in grade school I always had a lot of female friends compared to my guy friends.

I just like girls, what can I say?

Anyway, this girl and I never really gave romance a shot because when one of us was single, the other was not, until one summer when we both just magically happened to be single.

Back then I didn't really know that much about attraction. But my rapport game was strong because I liked having friends. And my attraction game was terrible because I was overly nice and compliant and ultimately I rarely took risks for fear of embarrassment or rejection.

I was a pussy, is what I'm trying to say, and I hadn't yet felt comfortable being a sexual male with sexual desire and I certainly didn't know how to express it.

Anyway, one day we're at her place alone, and she's making us some lunch in the kitchen, and up to this point I had decided I was growing a crush on her and figured I should tell her, with the hope and expectation that she would feel the same. (Movies had me all messed up about this. The romantic gesture of spilling our guts made sense to me.)

And so in her kitchen I started giving her this awkward but heartfelt little prepared speech about how she's pretty awesome and how I was having these new feelings for her and the whole time her body language was screaming *"Oh god no!"*. She was slowly backing away from me, and slowly shaking her head as an unconscious way of stopping me from embarrassing myself.

I could see I was losing her but I was committed to finishing what I was saying. My face felt hot and embarrassed but I continued.

I was horribly nervous going in, and my worst nightmare was coming true. I made a fool of myself.

She was polite about it, and very nice.

She said, *"Oh Robby, I really like you too but I'm not in that place where I can date someone new, especially a good friend, I don't want to ruin what we have, and I hope you understand."*

Blah blah blah. I wasn't really listening. I was so relieved to be done, despite the fact that I now had zero chance of being with her, and I felt this huge weight off my shoulders. I had made a big deal about this talk and once it was over I was relieved.

I think she was pretty relieved too actually, because I was cool with her not being into me.

I ultimately didn't care, because we were already friends. There was nothing to lose really. I did say to her though, as we both kind of laughed off the tension of that moment, *"You know, if you ever develop feelings for me, don't waste time give me an embarrassing speech like I just did, just come out and kiss me. Actually, to be honest, I wasn't even going to tell you, I just going to just kiss you. Gawd, what would you have done?!"*

And we both laughed nervously. And I was feeling so much better having had all that stress off my back, I really relaxed. And she said, *"Oh my god, I don't know what I would have done actually. And even if I was totally into a guy, there's just no way I would just come out and kiss him. I would just never do that."*

That's something I had never realized before, but it's true. It had never occurred to me that **women won't make the first move**. Even if they're super into a guy.

Do you hear what I'm saying?

Write that down and tattoo it on your forearm. No matter how into a guy she is, she's never going to make a move. **It's your job to take that risk**, even though ultimately it's not a risk.

So something happened to me that day after she explained that to me. Something about the relief I was feeling, and my happiness to be with this friend of mine, I was overwhelmed with how I felt about her. And so I suddenly had this amazing sense of confidence and courage that I hadn't had before.

And calmly, and confidently, I walked up to her, and took the pot out of her hand and placed it back on the stove, and I playfully backed her into the corner of her kitchen counter, so we were face to face, hip to hip, and I said, *"Well maybe we should just get the first kiss out of the way then, so you don't have to worry about it."*

And what was funny was that as she was backing up she was whispering, *"Oh no no no..."* but she was also kind of giggling and smiling.

It was confusing.

But honestly, I felt so confident and comfortable that I somehow was able to see past what she was saying in order to see how she was really feeling. And her body language seems comfortable with me being in her personal space. And basically I acted exactly like I would have with a woman I had been dating for years. I leaned my body into hers, and brought my face up to hers, and I gave her the space to decide for herself whether to kiss me, or push me away.

And I stood there in her personal space, with a serious look and a grin on my face, and I let her decide... and she stopped smiling and whispered, *"You smell so good..."* and then she leaned in to me slightly, and I met her halfway, and we made out for the first time.

I mean, this all happened within seconds, and I was just reading her body language. If I had the sense that she was uncomfortable with me being in her space, I wouldn't have leaned in on her like that.

So what's the moral of my story?

Don't waste time talking about your feelings.

Take action and move with integrity and confidence and you'll have the best chance possible at seducing her into being more than just friends.

There's a quote that goes, *"With confidence, you can get away with pretty much anything. If you think you cannot do something, there is no chance you can pull it off."*

It's not a guarantee, of course, but it's your best chance at something more.

MAKE A PLAN OF ACTION

Everything I've covered to this point has been to get you ready for the real task in this adventure, the one single reason you're in The Friendzone and not dating her: **escalation!**

Why haven't you tried kissing her yet?

You were scared of rejection?

You were scared of losing her attention?

You were scared?

But guess what?

There are really three possible outcomes if you try to make things happen with her:

1) She likes it and returns your interest.

2) She doesn't like it and feels flattered by your advances and you remain good friends.

3) She doesn't like it and feels you can't be friends anymore, which is actually very unlikely unless you shoved your hands down her pants.

Seducing a friend into a lover is a lot like boiling a live frog. You can't just toss her into a pot of boiling water, she'll jump out.

Instead, you must turn up the heat slowly so that she doesn't even notice until she's cooked. You must escalate your sexual relationship slowly (without stopping) so that she can feel comfortable with each stage.

In general, here's what you're going to do:

1) You're going to stop being the friendly doormat, and give her the gift of missing you.

2) You're going to get more educated on what attraction and seduction is, so that you have some new mindsets around how to act and behave with her.

3) You're going to lead all interactions with her moving forward.

4) You're going to go out and meet some new women, and go on some new dates, as a way of practicing your skills, and lessening your emotional attachment to this one girl.

5) You're going to take this girl out on a couple dates and finally kiss her beautiful little face.

Why is the goal just to kiss her face?

Because when you've made out, the rest is pretty much automatic.

I'm going to walk you through the specifics of what I would do, but it's your life, and you know your relationship best. If you think you need to escalate slower, like over three or four dates, then do that. Just realize that two dates is the most you really need.

You must think of this woman as any other woman you're dating. There's no need to drag your feet over 10 dates. That's too slow.

1) START DATING

Dating means you spend time alone doing things you would do on a date. The key here is to never refer to your time alone as a "date", because that puts your intentions way out there, and it puts pressure on her. Instead just call it nothing.

Remember, more action, less talky talk.

So line up a date.

For example, on the first date you take her to a fancy restaurant and then a nice walk afterwards, or if it's cold where you live, bounce to a lounge down the street after dinner for a drink and conversation. This second location within the first date makes it feel like two dates.

And for yourself, line up in advance where you want to take her to eat and drink, so that you don't have to ask her and you don't have to think about it on the day.

And prepare to have to pick her up and take her home. And prepare to have to pay for everything. You're taking her on a tiny adventure away from her real life, so this will cost you a little. Being a leader and being dominant and confident takes energy and effort. And she won't see this effort and she won't appreciate this effort. This is effort for **you** because you've decided this seduction is something you want. So expect to spend this energy and expend her to never appreciate it, although she may.

Then pick a non-busy night like a Wednesday (Friday nights and Saturday nights are fine, but you're risking her already being busy).

Then text her like this: *"Hey Susan, I'm busy Tuesday night and Thursday night, but I'd love to hang out with you this week to catch up. How about a little dining adventure with me Wednesday night?"*

Telling her the nights you're busy has plays a subtle role here. It helps her see you as busy and important. It's subtle and it matters. And make sure you really are busy the nights you've said you're busy, because she'll bring it up later. She might even be fishing to see if you're dating someone else.

She'll either say *"Sure"* or she'll say, *"I can't I'm busy, sorry."*

If she says no **and** doesn't offer another time she's free, that's a horrible sign. That's a sign you need to back burner her for another week. Don't text again. Don't ask if she's free the following Friday, etc. It's your job to read the signs. If she's interested at all, she'll offer another time. But she'll probably say *"sure."*

Remember, you're leading.

But also make it fun.

Say something like, *"Okay great, I'll pick you up at 6. Be sure to be hungry, wear something casual but sexy... like those tight jeans you have that I love so much. And comfy shoes for walking."*

She'll laugh and ask where the hell you're taking her. To which you say, *"It's a secret. But I promise you'll love it."*

It's perfectly okay to oversell and under deliver. The goal is to make sure she doesn't flake, and is super curious about where you're going.

2) TAKE HER ON THAT FIRST DATE.

It's your job to be clean, presentable and respectable. So be showered, shaved, and looking the best you've ever looked.

Get a haircut.

Buy new clothes.

Wash your car.

Clip your nails, trim your nose hair, ear hair, and ball hair.

And wear a tiny bit of cologne, so little that she will only be able to smell it if she's hugging you. Any more and it's way too much. Trust me.

When you pick her up, be sure to get out of your car, go around and let her in. Like a gentleman. Except give her a huge hug hello, like you've just gotten out of prison and you're so happy to see her.

And as a regular practice, I would recommend you get really good at hugging all your female friends hello and goodbye. Basically, get good at being touchy so that everyone gets used to it and comfortable with it.

What you're doing is escalating the touch.

She needs to get used to you two touching each other. Plus this helps her feel how strong you are (big hug) and how good you smell. Don't pussyfoot around with this hug. Lift her off her feet if it's not too weird. There's something women love about a hug. If you're a big guy that's even better. She needs to feel like you're big and strong and she's safe in your arms.

Next, drive to your restaurant and lead. That means helping her out of the car if possible by giving her your hand. And giving her your arm to hold if you're helping her up on the sidewalk, or around a puddle, or even through a crowd. You're looking for ways to lead her to the safety of your table. Even when the waitress takes you to your table, if it's possible to lead her by having her take your arm, do it. Be natural about it, like you're not even thinking, you're just doing it out of habit.

Like you're taking care of grandma or someone really special to you.

Now, I feel like it's okay to compliment a girl on how she looks, but only when it's sincere and only when you're doing it because it's on your mind, not because you're trying to impress her. For example, let's say you just hugged her hello, you might stand back and look her up and down like she looks delicious and you might say, *"Wow, you look great!"*

And take her hand and spin her around like you want to see her from behind, *"Yup, those jeans still fit you perfectly, nice work babe."*

Then move the conversation on. Don't linger on it or it'll turn creepy. You're letting her know that you find her yummy, and that you're not hiding it. Because you're comfortable being attracted to her, because she's attractive. **You have to treat her like you desire her.** And she can either take it or leave it. That's her business.

Next: Have a fun dinner.

Be normal.

Share stories.

Ask her about herself and her life and what's been going on. If she's dating someone, don't ask questions about it, just change the subject.

The point isn't to be jealous of who she's been with, it's to enjoy who you're with, in that moment.

That's your time together, enjoy it.

Drink her in.

And find ways to slowly escalate the touch. I go into way more details on escalation in my section on escalation in my *Get the Girl* video course (link at the back of this book), but here's some basics:

Find a reason to hold her hand, like walking through a crowd, or even better, looking at her nails. And then give her a fake palm reading. You're trying to get her used to your touch. Realize that how you hold and touch her hand will tell her everything she needs to know about how you'll be in bed.

Are you rough and uncaring?

Are you nervous?

Or are you strong but gentle, firm and with purpose while still being sensitive and caring?

I know it sounds like I'm exaggerating, but think about it. When you're into a girl and she casually touches your chest, or whispers in your ear, do you pay close attention?

Of course. We amplify everything someone does when we're into them. So she's doing that too when you hold her hand.

Plus it's like you're practicing being a leader. When you tell her to give you her hand, and she complies, that's you practicing being her leader. Telling her what to do and you showing her she'll enjoy herself when she does.

After dinner, bounce to another venue, like a casual lounge, where you can have a drink. (You're driving, so stick to tea or coffee, or prepare to Uber. That's okay too, but don't get drunk because you need to be on your A game. But it's okay if she gets drunk.) Sit side by side sharing stories and being close, slowly getting comfortable in each other's personal space.

You're slowly heating up the water.

Tell her a funny story, but pretend like you're too shy to let anyone hear the punch line so you have to whisper it in her ear, going in all slow kind of like you're going to bite her neck. And if the mood strikes, smell her neck, allowing your nose or lips to graze the skin on her neck, and lean back and say, *"Wow, you smell amazing, what is that?"* And then say, *"Come here, let me smell that again"* and lean in, forcing her to expose her bare neck to you again.

This is just you getting her used to letting you get close to her skin some more.

Now, if she's showing you signs of interest, and you kind of have a good vibe, then it's perfectly okay to kiss her at this lounge, if you're both having a blast and things heat up. This is why it's great to sit in a corner booth where you might have a little privacy.

If she lets you smell her neck a second time, and doesn't lean away when you lean in to enjoy how she smells, and maybe she gives a kind of cute moan, like it sort of gives her neck goose bumps to have you smell it, then you're golden.

Or if she's been asking way too many questions about who you're dating and keeps complimenting you on how you look and smell, then these are signs she's ready to be kissed.

And if this is the case, you might try something like this: lean in and say something too soft for her to hear, and stay leaned in grinning and she'll lean too and say, *"What?"* and then with confidence and a slight grin, say *"Give me a kiss"* and lean in slightly more like you're expecting her to kiss you.

I've done this many times and it works fine.

I've heard of other first kiss approaches, and they're all pretty good. Just search for "how to kiss close" on YouTube and you'll find a few good suggestions.

The key really is your confidence and reading her body language. When she's comfortable enough for you to lean in and play with her hair, while keeping flirty eye contact, and maybe you're looking from her eyes to her lips and back to her eyes, then she's ready to be kissed.

If she was uncomfortable with you in her personal space, she wouldn't let you near her face like that.

Now, she might lean in more and really want more of a kiss, in which case you give it to her. Or she might lean back in surprise and say *"What are you doing?"* to which you might lean back and laugh and say, *"I'm trying to kiss your cute little face!"*

And if she says, *"Whoa, why dude?"* just say, *"I was looking at you and I just suddenly really had this urge to kiss your face hole."*

What's important here isn't if she kisses you or not. It's how you handle her reaction to it.

Your job is to be so happy with yourself, and so confident, that you are proud that you tried to kiss her. You did all the right stuff. You waited patiently and you made your move.

You're officially a man.

So don't apologize.

Now, it's possible you misread her, and that's okay. That's how we learn. What you do next is what's important. You lean back like it's no big deal. If she's making a fuss, then just say, *"Hey, relax. It's okay, I misread you, and I wasn't expecting to want to kiss you. It's perfectly okay dude. I didn't realize you think it's so gross to kiss me, wow. Thanks."*

You're being playful, not actually upset.

Tease her about making a big deal out of nothing, then continue your night exactly how you were before. If she doesn't want the kiss, or you didn't have a good opportunity to kiss her, then line up another date the following week.

After you take her home, get out of your car and give her a hug and make sure she's home safe. I'm not big on trying to make the first kiss the goodnight kiss, but if you have a good vibe then feel free to go in for the kiss here.

I actually prefer not to do it. If I didn't have the balls to kiss her earlier that night I tend to wait for the next date. So I would just hug her and say good night.

Do not text her later saying you had a good time, unless it's in response to her texting you saying she had a great time. Go radio silent for a couple of days.

Repeat steps one through five again the following week. If you didn't have success on this first date, try again the following week, except this time have the date at your place. Make dinner together and watch some shows. Something like homemade pizza, or just a simple barbecue with some drinks. The booze helps everyone relax a little but isn't necessary.

The isolation of your place makes it a little more comfortable to make out anyway.

That's it. You follow steps one through five again. And you keep doing this, week after week, until you're either dating, or she's stopped accepting your date requests.

You should note, if you try to kiss her, and she gives you her cheek, that's fine! You both can giggle it off and let go of trying to kiss her again that night. **And here's the part that's important:** the following week, when you invite her over to your place for some food and entertainment and she agrees, she's basically saying she's open to you trying to kiss her again. Because no woman hangs out with a friend immediately after that friend tried to kiss her unless she's open to it.

I'll give you one last example from my experiences: back in the day, I was single and realized how hot one of my female friends was and I think she was starting to pick up on my vibe, but that didn't slow me down any, because she's fun to hang with either way. So I made myself a little weekend trip to another city, close enough to drive to.

And over some fast food I invited her to join me, and she said *"Sure, that would actually be a blast, but let me just give you some ground rules. This isn't some sex vacation, so no hanky panky mister."*

I agreed.

She gave me that boundary, and that's cool with me.

And after we crashed in our shared room, which had two beds, we sat in our PJs watching TV with pizza and beer. And as we settled in, we invented a game where the loser had to give the winner a back rub. Which is a great escalation technique that I think most guys are fully aware of already. I mean, a back rub is a great way to fondle each other. And sure enough, as we were settling into our beds she decided she'd come snuggle in mine, which gave me the green light to continue escalating... until we were both naked.

What I'm saying is, respect what she says, and realize that her mood dictates her choices more than her mind. So lead her emotions to a fun place, and she'll want to have fun.

STEP 5: ESCALATE

FINAL THOUGHTS

WHAT IF SHE'S STILL NOT INTERESTED?

Listen, every woman is different.

You can't seduce them all, that's impossible. And it's not your fault.

Doing nothing is your fault, of course, but if you're doing your best, and you're constantly escalating and being awesome, then it's really just that she's not that into you. **And there's nothing more you can do.**

Accept that she's a lost cause and just be awesome close friends anyway. **That's perfectly okay!**

Becoming the man this single woman desires requires you to be the man other women desire. And being able to let go of your attachment to just one woman is a **huge** part of growing up and becoming your healthiest, most handsome self!

How she feels about you has no real bearing on who you are, or what you're worth. This is something you must understand completely in order to be your best self! When your identity or self-esteem is tied to some outcome that you can't control (like this woman's desire for you), then you're already in a losing game that will fill you with despair and dread and shame and embarrassment. But if you tie your self-esteem and confidence to your deep inner belief that you were born worthy and will die worthy, then you're doing it right.

Your value is innate. From birth we are all perfect humans, no matter our flaws or mistakes. And the more deeply you realize this, the easier you will find it to let go of chasing women who aren't interested. Chasing leads to suffering. Letting go leads to peace of mind and the freedom to meet someone new!

The beliefs and skills within this book are applicable to any new girl you meet.

So go use your new superpowers for good!

And if you still want to be just friends, then just explain to her that you totally understand, and she can relax, you're not going to try to kiss her adorable little face again. You'll be good.

Stay playful, don't get weird, and don't get awkward.

Because there's no reason to.

MINDSETS

Remember that how you think about this girl, and your relationship with her, will impact how you will feel and therefore how she will feel.

So choose your thoughts carefully. And yes, we **can** choose what we believe.

This means that no matter how this plays out, you can still feel good about her and your relationship with her. You can choose to be okay being just friends. And you can choose to want more. And she can choose to share more, or not.

It's your job to be perfectly okay with any outcome that happens. Because life is too short to pout or feel rejected when one girl doesn't feel the same as you.

You can choose to accept that maybe things will never progress with her, while still enjoying how awesome and close you can be as just friends.

Think of Larry from Three's Company. The girls knew he was always trying to get into their pants, but he had fun with it (non-threatening). Basically, give yourself permission to be attracted to her, and to tease her and to flirt with her, with the carefree intent of a loving friend.

Of course, respect any boundaries she gives you. If she doesn't want you to kiss her or touch her, then don't. But it's perfectly okay to flirt and tease and enjoy each other's sexual energy without having to own each other, and without having to owe each other anything.

Most women will never be more than just friends. And that's okay. Think of the hundreds of women you pass on the street every week. How many would you even really want to see naked? Probably barely any of them. And therefore it's understandable that most women won't connect in the right way with us to be more than just friends. This is a fact of life and not a big deal. Because there are **so many women!**

Know, in your gut, that there is an abundance of choice out there and remind yourself of that every time you find yourself getting worked up over just one special girl.

Being "just friends" with a woman has so many other advantages over sex. There's honesty and connection and perspective and the female insights we wouldn't otherwise have access to if we didn't make friends with the opposite sex.

You can still enjoy the sexual energy she inspires within you without spending time fantasizing about getting her. This is also a healthy alternative.

It's a mistake to mull over a girl that's not interested in you, so make sure you don't do this. Mourn the loss if you have to, and let her go as soon as you can. It's harmful to fantasize in this way.

Plus you'd be amazed at how often people change their minds based on how they feel, so it's up to you to seduce her emotional body by leading and escalating.

That's it.

I wish you the breast of luck!

YOUR TOP QUESTIONS

QUESTION:

So I just got Friendzoned, and it sucks. The thing about the Friendzone is that it's basically a slap across my face, saying that I don't meet her level of sexual interest, or perhaps that she is just scared to damage our friendship.

It concerns me that the Friendzone is becoming a term of horrible rejection. It's like she's giving me sketchy hope, which I struggle with.

Why can't she just be real? Just say it! She should just break the friendship. She doesn't realize how awful friendzoneing is. It's materializing of her to seek some future boyfriend when the person right in front of her is showing her real and truthful love.

People should feel some sort of guilt when they Friendzone someone, because basically they're ignoring commitment while seeking something else, something more superficial. And I understand it is a consequence of being a human, that our bodies can be superficial or materialist.

But people should realize that they can't solve a materialistic problem with materialistic solutions. It's hard to understand how you can claim to be a friend who understands a person, but then friendzone them.

Maybe I'm just frustrated about being friendzoned, but I think I have a valid point here. What do you think? Do you think that when a person friendzones another that the person needs to accept responsibility for how it makes the other feel?

ROBBY:

Your ego is trying to make this all about you when it's got nothing to do with you. Our egos make us think everything everyone does is about us, and the immature side of you wants to blame her for "making" you feel rejected, as if she shouldn't reject you if YOU like her. As if she should be obligated to date you if you like her and you're already friends. That makes no sense!

When I was divorced (the first time, lol) I managed to meet a lot of beautiful women, all of whom I wanted to date and all of whom did NOT feel the same way. Somewhere along the line I was scaring them away.

At that time this felt like terrible rejection and complete confusion. I was good looking, funny and more importantly a super nice guy. This was how I saw myself anyway. I was ignoring the facts and overly focused on pointing fingers and seeking to blame others for my negative feelings.

Basically, I was frustrated and angry from the constant "rejection."

This frustration birthed my longstanding dating advice blog, FullOfHateAndReadyToDate.com. Needless to say, my anger and jealousy issues had nothing to do with the women I was trying to date and everything to do with my own issues and how my issues made me behave.

Remember: how you feel affects how others feel when they're around you.

I learned that when I was no longer insecure and needy, women suddenly wanted to date me instead of running away. The issues I was having weren't because of them, they were because of me. Once I took responsibility for how I was being, instead of trying to make these women responsible for how I was feeling (I stopped blaming them), then I recognized that it was ME that was the issue, and I turned things around for myself. You should do the same.

YOU are responsible for your feelings, your life, and your sexual success. Thinking like a victim, pointing fingers, and trying to blame others for how YOU feel will always leave you feeling shitty, weak and helpless.

With a little empathy, you'll realize that these women have every right to feel how they feel. And if they don't have a sexual interest in you, that's got nothing to do with you and everything to do with them.

Being your friend first does NOT imply they should also consider you a sexual option. Even kissing you, making out with you and sleeping with you do NOT commit them to being your girlfriend.

Just like you, all people have the option to change their minds about who they want to date, sleep with or be friends with. There is no obligation, spoken or otherwise, that ties us to each other.

Plus, how shitty would it feel to have a girl date you out of obligation instead of out of interest or love? It would feel terrible to see the look of unhappiness or disgust on her face each time you forced her to go on a date with you. Know what I mean?

But don't beat yourself up too much. It's perfectly normal to feel a little rejected when you're really into a woman, especially a woman who has already chosen you as friend material. That means you're awesome.

Just because she doesn't also want to sleep with you does NOT mean you're not worthy, or less than, or undesirable in some way. It just means SHE isn't feeling it. And it takes a little maturity and experience to disconnect your sexual value from the approval of women.

Just because one woman isn't into you or your genitals does not mean EVERY woman feels the same way.

Keep your chin up, make more female friends, and get out there and meet more women worthy of your time!

QUESTION:

This girl and I had been talking quite a bit and had started to get close. She seemed pretty interested in me so I decided to ask her out. She said "maybe" so I took it as a no.

Now she doesn't text or really talk to me but she also doesn't avoid me.

The last few times I saw her in person she looked over at me a decent amount and eventually she talked to me and joked around a little but it didn't last long.

This isn't her normal personality. She isn't a shy or awkward person.

The other day I posted a picture of my friend's puppy and she messaged me about dogs and what kind she wants to get. It isn't like she flat out ignores me. I usually see her a few times a week so I was wondering if I should confront her about the situation and try to make it better or should I do nothing and see if it fixes itself?

ROBBY:

Here's the thing: women are a mystery. Their insecurities are so different from ours that it's hard to see things from her point of view.

My advice would be this: continue to be fun, continue to flirt with her and continue to escalate.

Don't spend any time "talking" about why she's one way or another. A maybe is often a no, you're right, but not always.

Sometimes "maybe" just means "not yet."

So take that and work with it. Spend more time with her. Flirt, tease and be playful! Make her laugh. Make her enjoy her time with you.

And then invite her to join you on an adventure to some new restaurant or dessert place.

Don't be so formal.

Don't call it a date.

Just say, "Hey, there's this awesome new donut shop I've been dying to try, come with me this Thursday night after dinner! What time do you usual eat dinner? I'll swing by and pick you up after that..."

Or whatever seems natural for you.

You don't have to call these times together "dates". If she's super shy then she'll feel too much pressure. So instead go slow and slowly warm her up to your charm by spending time together without pressure.

What's the worst thing that could happen? It goes nowhere and you've made a nice friend? That's a pretty good payoff if you ask me.

FOLLOW-UP:

You're right. To make things more comfortable it all starts with me. I need to make her enjoy my company again. Maybe she is interested and maybe she isn't. I can't read her mind so I should keep escalating.

Best case scenario a relationship comes from it.

Worst case we don't communicate and avoid one another, similar to what's happening now.

Thank you, this helped!

QUESTION:

Okay, I've been friends with this girl for a couple months now. We hang out a couple times a week and we text every day. She's always flirting and stuff but she's always had a boyfriend so it's harmless. And last week they broke up. And I want her to be my girlfriend. Advice?

ROBBY:

If she's flirting already, then you're past Steps 1 through 4. Time for Step 5! ESCALATE!

Flirt. Tease. Be FUN! Get her alone. Have some drinks. Share secrets. Cuddle. Kiss her. Then have sex.

Having sex will pretty much close the deal because almost every girl wants to date the guy she's just slept with, unless it's a one-night-stand.

Reread Step 5 for some ideas on how to escalate. Or read my upcoming book entirely focused on escalation from the Get the Girl series.

Good luck and let me know how it goes!

QUESTION:

Help! I'm friends with this beautiful blonde. We met at work and have hung out like old buddies ever since. We go for dinners and text late into the evening.

Except she gives me advice on the women I'm dating and she tells me about the idiots she dates.

And now we're both single and I don't know why she's not making any moves or giving me any clear indications that I should make a move.

How do I let her know I'm into her?

ROBBY:

First, never tell her how you're feeling. The logic is a boner killer. Plus, she already knows; she's a woman after all.

I must say that you dating other women is a good move. That works heavily in your favour. Make sure that when you're talking about the women you date that you never complain about things and that you're never mean or rude about the women you date, because when you insult other women she will notice this. Plus, if you insult the women you date, what does that say about you? You're the loser who chose those women, after all.

Try to skip the sex stuff, unless you're explaining how these women keep saying you're amazing in bed, and that you're really opening them up to new stuff.

But mostly, don't spend too much time on the other relationships. If you want to grow this relationship, she's not going to want to imagine you banging other chicks so much. She just wants to know that you CAN if you want to.

And make sure she knows how selective you are. After all, you're a man of selection and choice, right?

Be more sexual. How much flirting do you two do? Because that needs to go up. She needs to feel like you're sexual and fun with her. She needs to feel that you're actually attracted to her and that you find her desirable. And that you're not ashamed of your desire for her, even if she's in a relationship. Be respectful, of course! But it's okay for her to realize you find her damn sexy in those jeans, and that she was super hot in that dress.

Next, be less predictable. Have your own opinions. Say NO more often. Leave things a mystery more often.

Make plans with her but don't give her specifics, just tell her what to wear to be comfy and to be hungry if you're going to feed her.

Don't always answer direct questions. Be playful. Don't always answer calls or texts. And sometimes hang out less. Be less available.

This spices up the relationship you have with her, and this is a good thing.

Remember Step 3? Lead more. If you're not leading then you're following. Make sure she sees your leadership qualities. When telling stories about you and your guy friends, make sure it's clear that you were leading them and not following them. This plays a big role in how she FEELS about you.

Finally, touch her more. This is all about escalation, Step 5, and it matters. She needs to be comfortable hugging you, play fighting, and otherwise being in close proximity to your touch.

We guys worry about touch too much. Respect her boundaries, don't grab her by the pussy, but also don't be scared of her or her body.

Things like fake palm readings in order to hold her hand.

Play games of chance where the loser has to give the other a back massage.

Piggyback rides.

Yoga together. Running together. Any exercise at all really.

Tickle fights.

Face painting each other.

Basically, let her know how good you are at touching her carefully but with strength and care.

All of this is a precursor to sex, so don't skip any of it!

And then escalate until you're making out!

QUESTION:

Can girls get Friendzoned or is this just something exclusive to guys?

ROBBY:

Yes of course, there are plenty of women who like guys but don't ever get any romantic traction going with them. But more often than not these women don't even know they're in the Friendzone officially.

Why?

Because most women will never take the steps that are required to get a guy to accept or reject them romantically in an overt kind of way.

We guys make moves, or we ask direct questions like, "So I like you, want to be more than just friends?" And then she can accept or reject his offer. This lets him know where he stands.

But most girls will NEVER take this step and therefore will never know FOR SURE where they stand, and therefore won't really know or care if they're always going to be just friends.

QUESTION:

I'm stuck in the Friendzone with two gorgeous women. TWO! What is wrong with me? Help!

ROBBY:

Stop thinking of the friendzone as a purgatory with no escape. Let's imagine that you follow all of the advice I have in this book and still these two "gorgeous" women don't want to blow you.

Then what?

Then you're stuck hanging out with two gorgeous women? Two women who you can watch interact with men, flirt, tease, accept or reject men?

These two women can be your BEST wingmen, teachers and mentors!

You can learn more from two hot women than you could ever learn from a book. So treat these women well, but not too well because you're not a pussy after all, and absorb every little piece of dating insight you can from them.

Let them help improve your dating profile. Your text conversations. The choices you make when choosing women. The clothes you wear. How you interact with women, etc., etc., etc.

Plus, you'll learn how to be comfortable around someone you want to bang without banging them. This alone is a great skill to develop. Instead of letting your dick make all your decisions, you might learn some control.

It's all good is what I'm saying. Don't dismiss this win!

QUESTION:

Isn't the Friendzone just a woman's insecure way of lying? Isn't she really wanting to say, "You're not attractive enough to want to have sex with, but I will accept all of the free attention you give me!" It feels like a lie. In truth, isn't the Friendzone just rejection?

ROBBY:

I can appreciate what you're trying to get at here. There is some truth to this. That women, when asked to be very specific and clear about their romantic feelings with a guy friend, are most likely to lie and say "it's not you, it's me" or "I don't want to risk our friendship with complications like sex." Because who wants to hurt someone's feelings when we don't feel the same sexual attraction they feel?

It seems like the lesser of two evils when we say, "Oh, it's not about you, it's about this other thing, so don't feel bad."

And as nice as it would be to point fingers at women and blame them for not loving us enough to have sex with us, and therefore everything they say is just a big lie to protect our sensitive egos (and yes, we guys can sometimes have very sensitive egos when it comes to acceptance and rejection), I suspect this term the Friendzone comes from a guy needing to explain away his own lack of sexual success with women. Like inventing the term "slut" is a way to counter the pain and suffering we feel with women choose other men over us.

The Friendzone probably has the same backstory. Some guys felt rejected and therefore made up a term to excuse themselves from the responsibility of their own sexual success. As if to say, "Oh, it's not about me or my inability to seduce this woman, it's really about her being superficial and making me just a friend."

Or maybe the Friendzone is actually a normal state of being for everyone until we're sleeping with them. Like waiting in the warmup area before going up to bat in a game of baseball.

Maybe the Friendzone is really just nothing. Like the moment before the first kiss. Sometimes that moment is months of hanging out and sharing. And sometimes that moment is the first few stressful hours of a first date.

Until that first kiss changes everything!

I'm saying, maybe we should stop worrying about the Friendzone like it's some type of judgement, and instead accept it as a normal stage of a relationship. The first and most important stage. The stage before all the excitement of sex. The stage where we get to relax and take it slow before we really have to shine and be vulnerable.

Let's enjoy this first stage, the Friendzone, and maybe not be in such a rush to escape it. I mean, sex is easy, and often over way too soon. But making friends? That's bloody hard. So appreciate it when it happens!

QUESTION:

Is there a difference between being in the Friendzone and just being friends?

ROBBY:

Typically, a guy who is in the Friendzone has an explicit sexual attraction that he wishes to act upon with his female friend and she doesn't reciprocate these feelings.

Being just friends implies that both parties have chosen not to explore a sexual or romantic relationship.

And I'll even add this: being just friends has the implication that the friendship is more "real" and authentic.

What is even more sad is that there is an implication that a guy in the Friendzone is inauthentic and is actually hiding his feelings for this girl.

While this may actually be true most of the time, my intent with this entire book is for guys who have romantic feelings towards their female friends to actively act upon those feelings, and at the very least not pretend they don't exist.

It is a mistake to "fake" being friends with a woman while secretly trying to sleep with her. This mostly shows itself in guys who act overly nice and put her up on a pedestal while hoping she appreciates his actions, gifts, attention and affection and will be inspired to return them in kind.

Except pretending to be nice or pretending to be someone we're not does NOT work. Being fake does NOT work.

The foundations of this book are about being authentic. If you're attracted to a female friend, that's okay! There's no need to hide those feelings. You will always have to act within the boundaries of respect and kindness, but you don't have to pretend you're not horny or sexually charged when around someone who's hot.

We guys too often feel shame for our sexual energy. I'm saying DON'T feel shame. But also don't abuse this sexual attraction as a reason for acting like an asshole or an immature masturbating bear.

The kind of man women are ultimately drawn to are men worthy of being friends with first, let's be honest. If he's someone worth hanging out with, AND he can be himself, AND he can be flirty and attractive, that's the best combo.

The trick is to have a spine or a backbone when that hottie makes requests of you. The "nice guy" will let her walk all over him, and this is a turn-off for women.

That's why I suggest we men take responsibility for our feelings and our lives. If we want a woman, we act on it, with pride, care and authenticity. And if it pushes her away, that's okay, because we can walk away knowing we were our best selves, instead of hiding our feelings and feeling regret.

Being just friends implies that there SHOULD be more, but look at our same-sex friendships. They are typically our best friends. Are those friendships less because we're not blowing each other? I'd like to say no. I'd like to think we're still our best selves even if there's no romance or sex.

Anyway, that difference is that one partner has a sexual interest that the other doesn't share...yet! Hehehe.

QUESTION:

Is it considered mean if I don't wish to stay in her Friendzone? I feel humiliated enough being designated to the Friendzone so I'd rather just not. Is this wrong?

ROBBY:

Feeling humiliated is a pretty big stretch, isn't it? Humiliated is when you're video recorded masturbating to animal porn and it's shared on Facebook with your extended family. Having a girl not want to sleep with you is 95% of all men's dating reality.

Letting yourself think that it's embarrassing or humiliating when a girl doesn't fall in love with you is a super dramatic stretch and not reality, so maybe let go of the fiction you're writing about yourself and your situation. Let's get back to reality a little bit here.

As for your real question, is it okay to move on? Yes, of course!

If you're super into her and she's just not feeling the same, then of course it's okay to move on. Letting her go, if that's what you need, is perfectly acceptable. Especially because it frees you up to go out and meet more women.

I can appreciate that having a hot female as a friend has advantages, but if you're too wrapped up in her, then YES, cut her free (with kindness and respect, of course) and move on. I would NOT recommend you pout and push her away like a child sulking. Don't be a baby.

Remind yourself that you're an awesome guy who doesn't get upset about not getting his way, and with care let her know that you appreciate how awesome she is but that you're not comfortable just hanging out when you have these feelings for her, so you'd rather let her go so that you can focus on yourself while allowing yourself the freedom to meet someone new.

Good luck!

QUESTION:

Is the Friendzone permanent? I've heard that once a girl feels a certain way about a guy there's nothing you can do to change that. Is this a lost cause?

ROBBY:

How she FEELS about you is sometimes like the weather. It's ever changing and often surprising.

If you want to seduce her from a friend into a lover, you're going to have to BE a different guy. You're going to have to DO different things. So that when she's around you she literally FEELS differently.

I've outlined your best changes for success in these five steps, so follow them as best as you can, and always be learning new things about women and dating. Read online, buy my book Ignore and Score and learn as much as possible.

Because to get new results with her, you're going to have be a new man, someone who's attractive, fun, a leader, and willing to escalate!

QUESTION:

How do I tell if I'm in the Friendzone?

ROBBY:

When you go to escalate the romance of the relationship, either in a big way or a small way, and she stops you and says, "I just want to be friends", that's how you know.

BUT if she stops you but doesn't say anything about "just being friends", that just means "not right now." So if you were trying to hold her hand or kiss her but she stopped you, this just means she's not yet ready.

Read Step 5 regarding escalation. When she stops you, take two steps back and then slowly start escalating again until she stops you again.

Never get upset, always play it cool, and relax.

Don't rush.

Be patient.

Seduction is to be enjoyed, not rushed!

SPECIAL THANK YOU

As a reminder... I'm new at this writing stuff. Creating this book has been challenging but fun!

I really enjoyed the process, but I also recognize that I'm no natural at teaching or delivering content. **So please contact me with your dating questions and your course suggestions!**

I can handle criticisms, especially if it helps you with your love life.

Also, please participate in any student discussions. We men should help each other!

Positive book reviews are extremely important to me. Writing this book to help men is part of my livelihood, and positive reviews lets Amazon know that they should continue to promote the visibility of this book, **so if you can try to remember to leave an honest review**, it would be **much appreciated!**

Email me: _robert@bobair.com_